Bits & Baubles

Corey Grant

BookLeaf Publishing

India | USA | UK

Made with ❤ on the BookLeaf Publishing Platform
www.bookleafpub.in
www.bookleafpub.com

Dedication

To My Wife,

You are the only audience I want to impress. Everything I write is for you.

Preface

Dear Reader,

Before you dive into *Bits & Baubles*, let's clear the air—
yes, the poems within may feel like they've been penned
by a morose soul trapped in a dingy attic. I have verses
that flirt with melancholy and occasionally throw an
angsty tantrum. Some may even appear as bleak as a
Monday morning without coffee.

But outside these pages, I'm quite cheerful. I laugh at bad
puns, enjoy a sunny day, and sometimes even whistle
while doing the dishes. This collection isn't a mirror of
my daily existence but rather a repository of moods and
musings that demanded their moment on paper.

So, sit back, sip something warm (or something stronger,
no judgment here), and take a peek. I promise, though
the path may seem a bit grim, there's always light at the
end of the stanza.

Happy reading—or brooding, if that's your thing.

Warm regards,
Corey Grant

Acknowledgements

To my wife, my queen and editor of my comma splices—thank you for your endless patience and your keen eye for all things poetic (and prosaic).

To my family, who have always been my biggest cheerleaders—even when my poems left them scratching their heads—none of these poems are about you (and that's a good thing).

To my friends, who listened, nodded, and occasionally offered a polite "Interesting..." - thanks for pretending to enjoy my impromptu poetry readings.

And finally, to the masters like Cohen, Bukowski, Oliver, and other writers who I could not come close too in sheer artistic creativity—thank you for sharing your writing with us.

This collection is for all of you, the true baubles in my life.

Fairground

Here's your ticket
Hope on a ride
The grass might be greener
on the other side.

It's all a circus,
a messed-up show.
Face the sad clowns,
honk the red nose.

Eat all the food -
It's salty,
it's fried.
Throw it all up;
at least we say we tried

Find some cool shade.
Enter a humid tent.
The tattoo man is selling -
Holy oil with peppermint.

The shadows stretch.
The sun is falling.
Capture the music -

When the notes are still moving.

There's one way to leave,
only one way outside
Look for the entrance,
and run back inside.

An Apology Note to the Sun

I miss you, sun.
I said I prefer
clouds.
But I admit -
I was wrong.
Please come back -
My toes are numb.

Who Is On the Other Side of the Door?

Who
is on the other side of the door?
It looks like me,
standing in the rain -
Sad, grim, and grimy.

But it couldn't be me,
on the other side of that door.
For I am laying here,
naked on the kitchen floor.

So what remains outside
on the the other side of this door?
A man.
A beast.
A flower -
Budding in a hardware store?

Take another peek
at the thing on the other side.
Stare into the peephole
at the presence you can't ignore.

An eye looks back at you,
from the other side of your door.
Now you see what you cannot miss -
Looking back is the blackened shore.

Destruction

Devoted to destruction.
Deaf to instruction.
Running to failure.
Continuous compulsion.

Devoted to destruction.
Committed to nothing.
Lighting the matches.
Expanding explosion.

Devoted to destruction.
Loyal to lamentation.
Couldn't stop if I tried -
Frightening frustration.

Devoted to destruction.
Unwavering expectation.
Every choice is wrong.
Damning determination.

In Lainey's Car

In Lainey's car
the blue seat covers
are worn and faded
soaked by the hot
Texas sun.

On the floorboards,
a collection of shoes;
each in varying stages
of thermodynamics.
Each pair a snapshot
from Lainey's unfinished biography

The flip-flops
from her life in California.
The wicker loafers
from her stint in Honduras.
The scuffed high heels
from her excursions to
middling bars and restaurants,
to match with other pairs of shoes,
and maybe a bed
to crawl underneath
and call home for awhile.

Lainey's backseat
is her closet.
You can find wrinkled blouses
and holey jeans
and stained hoodies
and skirts
and socks
and lacy panties
and 5-year-old bras
and other things
to cover up or take off.

It is a pioneer's wagon -
rambling across wide open
places, braving the wild
and loving the journey.

I grab her hand
across the dusty console.
I hold on.
It is good to be in Lainey's car.

Hurry Up to Nowhere

Pockets full of empty,
walking down the street.
Livin' is expensive -
But dying sure is cheap

Hurry up to nowhere,
the preacher man isa cheat.
Lyin' comes real easy
with an acolyte in the sheets

This bottle of bourbon is full
when you look at the glass just right.
You'll always win the battle
if you never join the fight.

Your tone is much too somber -
Try writing something bright!
He's holding back your good
So c'mon ... take a bite

Eat!
Drink!
Be merry!
It all ends some day.

Knowing it's temporary
makes everything okay.

Identity

I am

    my name
    on a plastic
    credit card

Buying
    shiny things
    I have no use for

I am

    my name
    on a white
    envelope

crammed
with offers
for stuff I can't afford

I am

    my name
    on a silly

little rhyme

scratched
on clean paper
to help pass the time.

Hairs

Another hair
fell out.

Only
10,317,615 left.

Should I be worried?

Long Road Trip

We pull up
to some shitty diner
on the corner of
Pike and First.

You pull down
you sun visor
and study yourself
in the mirror
while looking through
your purse.

You sweep
your bangs around
and put another
coat on your lips.

I don't want to leave
the car. It's beautiful
right here.
Escaping with you
on a long road trip.

We go inside,

find a beaten corner booth.
I order a beer
and you get pancakes
for two.

I push food around
my plate -
hungry, but not for
what's here.
Tracing with my eyes
the movement of your fingertips.

Escaping with you
on a long road trip.

Ink In My Glass

Though the evening has fallen
the sun is still up
Should I hurry on back?
Or race to catch up?

The clatter of pans.
A hiss from the stove.
The smell of chopped garlic
wafting towards my nose.

I know that a meal
is being made.
But I need some time
to get fed another way

To drink in rich solace.
To munch on salty thoughts.
I digest the day,
before it molds and rots

This is my dinner -
A fulfilling repast.
The plate full of paper
with ink in my glass.

Dirty Rug

I laid on the floor.
My weary muscles
melting into
a dusty, second-hand rug.

You laid beside me
pushing your body
against me,
as if you wanted to
crawl inside my skin.

And I feel guilty
because I've never
wanted someone so badly.
Maybe I have a defect,
like a factory shoe
with no tongue
or a shirt sewn
with three arms.

Your hair is underneath
my chin now,
and I smell coconuts
and stifled dreams

and poignant problems

I wonder
"how long should I do this
before I stop?"
But my fear of ... what? is
heavier than my love
and so I stay -
glued to a dirty rug
and a clean you.

When...

When...
Pigs fly.
When birds spin
woozy webs.
When baking cookies
smell like rubber fires.
When Satan ice skates with angels
and sips hot cocoa after.
When jazz hits all the right notes
and Theolonius forgets to count
4/4 time.
When the shadows grow long
and overwhelm the sun.
When the universe is folded
into a dinner-napkin swan.
When all that we've learned
is lost to eternity
and only the vapor of knowledge
hovers over the dried-up sea.
Then...
my love for you will stop -

But not one second before.

Please Don't Close the Door

The engine is idling.
Your foot on the brake.
I ran out,
 no shirt and bare foot,
and many years too late.

Your bags in the trunk
and tears in your eyes.
The driver door open,
You sitting there
saying good-bye.
And me, holding on for dear life.

I get it.
I understand now.
The pain
I caused.
The loneliness you felt.
You wanted me
to open up -
And I chose to shut you out.
If you leave me now
I'll know exactly what for.

But baby, I'm begging,
Please don't close the door.

I watched my mom
stand outside his trailer door.
A woman's shadow behind
the glass -
A scene we've all seen before.
My mother is crying.
My father is silent -
One hand on the knob,
running from his pain

I get it.
I understand now.
The pain
I caused.
The loneliness you felt.
You wanted me
to open up -
And I chose to shut you out.
If you leave me now
I'll know exactly what for.

But baby, I'm begging,
Please don't close the door.

Super Villain

If my bank account
had more zeros
than a donut shop
I would become
a raving megalomaniac.

My host of flying monkeys
would build my underground lair,
where in dark seclusion,
listening to Vivaldi
and drinking 60-year-old Scotch,
I would hatch sinister plans
for world domination.

Sometimes I would take
a break
and listen to a podcast
about breathing through your nose
to relive stress.
But after it ends -
right back to nefarious stratagems.

I hope I would be
a benevolent dictator -

But one can never know.
So I play the lottery
and clench sweaty slips of paper
between my potentially evil fingers
and hope for enough money
to make me a super villain.

Holy Stones

The holy stones lay
scattered
at the head of
every street.

The holy roller's laughter
echo
from each
hidden piece.

Keep your voice
down
lest the wolves
come out to eat.

It's the same
air
whichever nostril
you breath.

I have tasted
ashes
and found them
to be sweet.

Tuck the
children
into bed -
It's time for all to sleep

Buy a blueberry
at fifty dollars
and keep
the receipt.

The holy stones are
empty -
stare into
the void of conceit.

I Would Kill for You

I would kill for you...

Murder my pride.
Destroy my fear.
Unalive my anger.
Kill my greed.
And bury
the worst parts of me.

I would kill for you.

Bug In A Shoe

I woke up
feeling like a cricket
in a dirty tennis shoe.

Went about my day
like a zombie with
an existential headache.

Sat down
to a frozen page -
thoughts just below the surface
but too submerged to
float to the top.

I went outside,
to a world on fire
sanctified soot falling
down on proverbial prodigals
dining on seed pods
and thinking
they're French macaroons.

A veiled sun
shines upon my face,

like a prophet
fresh off a call
with the Divine.

I mix my metaphors
in a wheelbarrow
full of concrete
hoping it sets into a solid
truth (or at least
an amusing anecdote).

But I am still a bug in a shoe
So what can I do?

Cisterns

A broken well.
My kitchen sink.
Blood pours out
when I want to drink

Sweat seeps out
as I dig a ditch.
Looking for water
from the belly of a fish.

My strength!
My power!
My mind!
My hour!

But it's the cisterns
I did not hollow
that always provide
the sweetest water.

Looming Precipitation

A tenebrous sky
and a quivering hand.
I had a bad start
but I'll do it again.

Looming
precipitation

Gave it all I had,
but it wasn't enough.
Now I'm walking under ladders -
Seven years of bad luck.
And I'm wishing
I could rent
all of my stuff

Looming
precipitation

The rain is falling
but my eyes remain dry.
Could have made it work
but you didn't want to try.
And these tears will drop,

but under false guise.

Looming
precipitation.

Streets of Seattle

I meandered
my way
through the moss-covered
pavement of Seattle
looking for
a steamy black cup
of coffee
and a quiet place
to contemplate
life, and the universe,
and other small oddities.

On Capitol Hill, I brushed
past a mother
pushing a
sleeping toddler
in an over-priced stroller.
I nodded a "hello",
silently, as to not
wake a dreaming babe
who was likely conjuring
a place
where cats talk
in husky tones

and handfuls of sweets
grow on every
city bush
and mom and dad
love each other
and kiss goodnight
and maybe slap
each other on the bottom -
dreaming of a place
where he was once was
or else
how could he remember
it so clearly?

It's a place I'm
looking for
and so is my
friend, who sticks
a bloody needle in his arm
there on the streets of Seattle.

Nepenthes

In a world of difficult
I need some ease.
A room full of "no thank you"
I want to hear "please."
Captive by thoughts
I long to be free...

Drink in
Nepenthes.

One of you
adds up to three.
Never alone
'cause I always live with me.
Cast down your weapons
let's end it peaceably...

Drink in
Nepenthes.

Escape yourself -
Imagined fantasy.
Rip the curtains down
covering communal holies.

Laugh at the king
in all his naked finery...

Drink in
Nepenthes.

Carry me out to sea.
Talk gently to the coral,
dying quite patiently.
Sadness lives too long,
speaking metaphysically...

Drink in
Nepenthes.

9 789369 544684